DATE DUE		

DRUG DANGERS

CRACK AND COCAINE

DRUG DANGERS

Paul R. Robbins, Ph.D.

Enslow Publishers, Inc.

44 Fadem Road	PO Box 38
Box 699	Aldershot
Springfield, NJ 07081	Hants GU12 6BP
USA	UK

http://www.enslow.com

*The author would like to thank
Dr. Sharon Hauge, George Lane, and Martha Weaver,
for contributions to the manuscript.*

Library of Congress Cataloging-in-Publication Data

Robbins, Paul R. (Paul Richard)
    Crack and cocaine drug dangers / Paul R. Robbins.
    p. cm. — (Drug dangers)
    Includes bibliographical references and index.
    Summary: Examines the social, medical, and legal aspects of crack and
cocaine, the effects of their abuse, and different treatment programs.
    ISBN 0-7660-1155-0
    1. Cocaine habit—United States—Juvenile literature. 2. Crack
(Drug)—United States—Juvenile literature. [1. Crack (Drug)
2. Cocaine. 3. Drug Abuse.] I. Title. II. Series.
HV5825.R58   1999
362.29'8—dc21   98-30271
                                                CIP
                                                AC

Printed in the United States of America

10 9 8 7 6 5 4 3 2 1

To Our Readers:
All Internet addresses in this book were active and appropriate when we
went to press. Any comments or suggestions can be sent by e-mail to
Comments@enslow.com or to the address on the back cover.

Photo Credits: © Copyright 1997, 1996 T/Maker Company, pp. 24, 34, 35;
Díamar Interactive Corp., pp. 6, 14, 45; Library of Congress, p. 18; National
Archives, pp. 9, 16, 19, 21, 26, 32, 39; National Library of Medicine, p. 48;
Steve Pecoraro, p. 29.

Cover Photo: National Archives

contents

introduction

A 911 call brought the rescue squad. The paramedics performed cardiopulmonary resuscitation (CPR), the life-saving method of applying pressure to the chest and breathing into the mouth. But it was no use. They could not revive Len Bias. The rising young basketball star had died after snorting cocaine.

Len Bias grew up in the Washington, D.C., area. It is an area where many young boys play basketball—their favorite sport. Some of these boys have gone on to become college stars. Some have even gone on to stardom in the National Basketball Association (NBA). Len grew into a very tall, strong young man. As others before him had done, he worked hard to develop his skills on the basketball court. He was a star on his high school basketball team. Then he went to the University of Maryland, where he was an outstanding player. When the day came for the NBA draft of college players, Bias was one of the top picks. The Boston Celtics made him their number one selection. A rewarding and exciting career as a professional basketball player lay ahead.

After his selection by the Celtics, Len Bias flew to Boston. He held a press conference and met the other players on the team. He even signed a contract to do commercials for an athletic shoe company. It was a dream come true. He was a gifted athlete who had worked hard to become one of the best young basketball players in the nation.

Many young people play basketball, but few are selected to play in the National Basketball Association, as Len Bias was.

When Bias returned home from Boston, he met an old friend. They decided to celebrate. They bought a six-pack of beer and a bottle of cognac. They asked two of Bias's teammates to join them. Then the group went to Bias's room on the university campus. They had the six-pack and the cognac to drink. They also had an ounce of cocaine.

During the party, Bias snorted the cocaine and had a seizure, a sudden attack. He stopped breathing. It was all very sudden. No one expected anything like this to happen. But it did. Len Bias, up-and-coming young basketball star, was dead.[1]

The death of Len Bias was a big story. During the nine months following his death, the *Washington Post* published more than four hundred articles about the case.[2] The tragic death of Len Bias was one of the stories that heightened public awareness about the rising problem of cocaine abuse.

Cocaine is a double-edged sword. On one hand, it offers the user moments of euphoria—feelings of alertness, energy, and high spirits. On the other hand, its effects are highly unpredictable (as was the case with Len Bias), and it is highly addictive. For some users, it becomes the focal point of their lives. However, cocaine and crack can do serious harm to the body. As was true in the case of Len Bias, it can kill.

one

Society and Cocaine

Cocaine is not a new drug. In the early sixteenth century Spanish conquerors in South America saw natives use coca leaves. Cocaine was "discovered" around 1860 by German chemists.[1] They removed the drug from the leaves of the South American coca plant. For centuries before that, however, native peoples of Bolivia and Peru had chewed the leaves of the coca plant. They found that chewing or sucking the coca leaves gave them extra energy when they were tired.

When cocaine was discovered, the drug became very popular and was widely used. It was generally thought that cocaine was safe to use and might have health benefits.[2] People snorted cocaine powder through their noses. Cocaine was also used in ointments thought to kill pain and put into tonics.

In time, experience with cocaine led doctors

and scientists to change their minds about the drug. Cocaine did not have health benefits. In fact, it was viewed as addictive and dangerous. Laws that greatly restricted the sale and use of cocaine were passed in 1908 and 1914 in the United States. In time, cocaine use declined.

Tracking cocaine use in America is like watching the waves in the ocean. Cocaine use has risen, declined, then risen again. In the 1920s, cocaine use was described as "an epidemic."[3] Then use fell, only to increase again in recent times. During the 1980s, new forms of cocaine were developed. These new forms made cocaine use more widespread and an even more serious public health problem. These new forms of cocaine are called freebase and crack. Freebase and crack cocaine are smoked. Powdered cocaine is sniffed into the nostrils.

Powdered cocaine (shown here) is sniffed into the nostrils. Freebase and crack cocaine, which are smoked, have quicker, more powerful effects than powdered cocaine.

Freebase and crack have quicker, more powerful effects than powdered cocaine. Crack, in particular, is very inexpensive to produce. Due to its accessibility, it has become a major concern for people working in public health and law enforcement.

Cocaine Use Today

How many people in the United States have tried cocaine or crack? Do most of these people become regular users? What kinds of people tend to be cocaine users? Researchers have studied such questions by conducting surveys. They have knocked on the doors of American homes to ask about drug abuse. They have also gone into schools. Students have filled out questionnaires about drug abuse.

The studies tell us that many millions of people have tried cocaine. Most of these people, however, have not become regular users.[5] Unfortunately, there is a flaw in these surveys. There are many cocaine users who do not ever show up in these surveys. For instance, homeless people and young people who have either dropped out of school or never attended school are not counted.

People between the ages of twenty-six and thirty-four have the highest rate of trying cocaine at some point in their lives. About one in five adults in that age range has tried the drug. Men are more likely than women to have used cocaine.[6]

Teenage Cocaine Use

The idea that most teenagers are using crack and cocaine is simply not true. Most teenagers do not use cocaine in any form. What is true is that *some* teenagers use

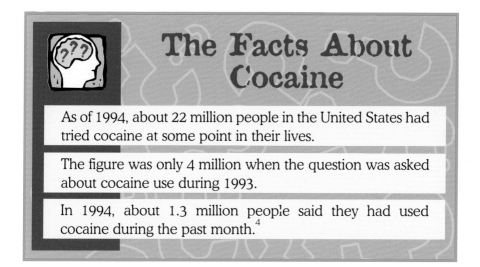

The Facts About Cocaine

As of 1994, about 22 million people in the United States had tried cocaine at some point in their lives.

The figure was only 4 million when the question was asked about cocaine use during 1993.

In 1994, about 1.3 million people said they had used cocaine during the past month.[4]

cocaine. The numbers increase as students go through high school.

Denise Kandel and Mark Davies are researchers at Columbia University in New York. They conducted a study of teenage crack users. They found that these teenagers did not feel as close to their parents as did teenagers who were not crack users. Crack-using teenagers tend to be involved with their friends. And many of these friends also use crack. Nearly four out of ten of the teenage crack users studied reported that crack or cocaine was used by most or all of their friends.[9]

Kandel and Davies also found that the crack users they studied were not doing well in school. Their grades tended to be lower than those of students who did not use drugs. They did less homework and were more likely to be absent from school. They were also more likely to be involved in stealing and serious fights at school.[10] Kandel and Davies reported that crack-using teenagers were sometimes picked up by police for driving when high. One of the tragic facts about cocaine is that its use

Teens and Cocaine

As of 1995, about 4 percent of eighth-grade students had tried cocaine. (That's about one child in a typical classroom.)

As of 1995, about 6 percent of twelfth-grade students had tried cocaine. (In a high school graduating class of three hundred students, that would be about eighteen students.)[7]

A great deal of publicity has been given to crack. Still, most teenagers seem to steer clear of it. Only about three in one hundred teenagers report they have ever tried crack.[8] (However, it is possible that these figures may not be entirely accurate, because some teens may not be truthful in reporting their usage.)

has been linked to fatal automobile accidents. In New York City, it was reported that recent use of cocaine was detected in nearly 18 percent of persons who were killed in car accidents.[11]

Medical Emergencies

Cocaine and crack are unsafe drugs. Their use has led to large numbers of medical emergencies. Overdoses of these drugs are common. Some of these overdoses have been fatal. Cocaine use is more often involved in people rushing to hospital emergency rooms than is any other illegal drug. In 1994, there were more than 142,000 emergency room incidents involving the use of cocaine or crack in the United States.[12]

Crack Babies

A woman always has a choice about whether or not to use crack. When she is pregnant and uses crack, however, the developing baby has no choice. He or she will be affected by the woman's decision. A 1994 study indicated that about forty thousand pregnant women used crack cocaine. Babies born to crack-using mothers have a higher risk of premature births and lower birth weights. Many of these babies will be kept in the hospital for extra care. Researchers continue to study crack babies—babies born to crack-addicted mothers. They hope to see how the babies' exposure to cocaine affects their development. Reports show that these children have problems focusing their attention. They also tend to have more behavior problems than other children.[13] Children who are not crack babies but are exposed to heavy crack smoking (being in the same room as the smoker) may show seizures and unsteadiness.[14]

The Penalties for Using and Selling Cocaine and Crack

Using or selling cocaine in any form is a crime. There are state, federal, and international laws against using and providing cocaine. If you are picked up by the police with even a very small amount of the drug, you are likely to end up before a judge. If you are picked up with larger amounts of cocaine or are caught selling it, you could end up with a long prison sentence.

At the present time, the penalties for possessing significant amounts of crack (more than five grams) are much more severe than those for possession of powdered cocaine. Statistically, African Americans have

Pregnant women who choose to use crack also choose to affect their developing babies. Babies born to crack-using mothers have a higher risk of premature births and lower birth weights.

been the ones most often arrested for crack-related (and other) offenses. They have also had to face longer prison sentences.[15] The fairness of having a much stiffer sentence for possession of crack than for powdered cocaine was questioned in a recent court case. A man, a decorated Gulf War veteran, was caught selling drugs to an undercover police officer. The man's lawyers said he had no criminal record. He had just gone along with the drug seller as a bodyguard and driver. He pleaded guilty to one count of distributing crack. Because there were more than fifty grams of crack involved, the man was sentenced to a minimum of ten years in prison. If the drug had been powdered cocaine, instead of crack, it would have taken five thousand grams of the drug to draw the same ten-year sentence. The man's lawyers appealed his sentence all the way to the United States Supreme Court. They claimed that it was unfair to have such different penalties for crack and powdered cocaine. The Supreme Court refused to hear the case.[16]

Efforts are being made in Washington, D.C., to change the law. Many believe that the penalties for using cocaine and crack should be made more equal. At the present time, however, laws against possessing crack are very severe. A person caught with five grams of crack faces a possible prison sentence of at least five years for a first offense.

Crime, Cocaine, and Crack

In some ways the involvement of criminals in the distribution of cocaine and crack is similar to what happened with alcohol in the 1920s. For many years, people worked hard to make producing and selling alcohol illegal in the United States. When at last they

Penalties for possessing significant amounts of crack (more than five grams) are much more severe than those for possession of powdered cocaine.

succeeded, there was great joy among them. Their joy was short-lived, however. The demand for alcohol remained high, and people began to make alcohol illegally. Prohibition (the period in United States history when making, drinking, or selling alcohol was illegal for everyone) provided an opportunity for criminals to make big money. Criminal mobs went into business. One of the best known of these mobsters was Al Capone. His gunmen fought other mobs on the streets of Chicago to gain control of the territory.

The drug lords of today operate in somewhat different ways from the mobs of the 1920s. However, the basic principles involved are similar:

1. There is a high demand for drugs.
2. Drugs are illegal.
3. There are always people willing to supply the drugs.

Cocaine and crack found in the United States often come from South America. They often pass through Mexico and end up on the streets of New York, Los Angeles, Washington, D.C., and other towns and suburbs. Then suppliers provide them to local dealers who sell them to users. Terry Williams is a sociologist who studied the drug trade in New York City in the 1980s. He found that the local drug dealers preferred to operate in abandoned, rundown buildings in poorer neighborhoods.

The members of the drug ring that Williams studied were all teenagers. The head of the group bought cocaine from a supplier. That supplier had connections to drug suppliers in Colombia, South America. The other members of the teenage drug ring sold the drug to customers in the drug ring's office or on the street. They worked hard to hide their drug dealings. One girl in the group hid cocaine in her bra.

Being a member of a drug ring is a very risky business. One member of the drug ring Williams studied was arrested and sent to prison. Another member was shot during a supposed drug buy that turned into a robbery.[17]

Young people, even neighborhood children, are sometimes recruited into the drug-selling business. There is the lure of making a large amount of money quickly, and young people under a certain age get lesser sentences and lesser criminal records for their crimes than adults. However, the risks are high. The chances of running into an undercover officer are always present.

The involvement of criminals in the distribution of cocaine and crack is, in some ways, similar to what happened when alcohol was made illegal during prohibition in the United States.

Large numbers of young men and women are now behind bars for cocaine- and crack-related convictions. The high risks of selling cocaine are clear.

There are other tolls on the community. Illegal drug markets can make life unpleasant and dangerous for the great majority of law-abiding people in these neighborhoods. Violence that can erupt between drug sellers has taken innocent victims. People who happen to be in the wrong place at the wrong time have been gunned down. Innocent children have been the victims of stray bullets—often the result of drug deals gone bad. Crack houses, where users spend their time smoking

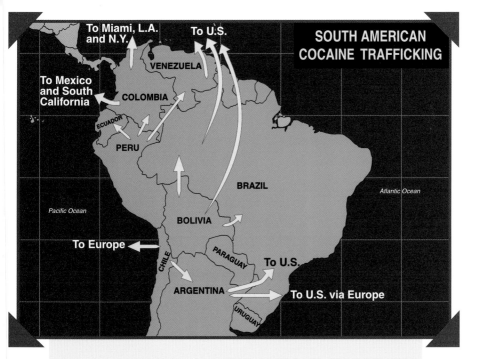

This map shows some of the ways in which cocaine is shipped from South America to a variety of other destinations, including the United States.

Current Penalties for Trafficking of Cocaine (1997)[18]

Offense	Penalty
First: For powdered cocaine (500 to 4,999-gram mixture For crack (5 to 49-gram mixture)	Not less than five years nor more than forty years
Second: For powdered cocaine (500 to 4,999-gram mixture For crack (5 to 49-gram mixture)	Not less than ten years nor more than life

Note: There have been discussions about changing the penalties for crack.

crack and freebase cocaine, are another symptom of a neighborhood infested with cocaine and crack. Terry Williams visited more than one hundred crack houses in New York City. He described them as having "a stark unattended look."[19] They were drab places with lookouts sometimes posted just inside the door. About ten to twenty people would come on a given night to use freebase cocaine. They smoked it in glass pipes. Williams reported that the people were more or less constantly stoned.

Williams described some of the people who used the crack houses. One of the young women was known as T. Q. She was a quiet person who dressed in jeans and a man's shirt. She did not wear makeup and had a boyish look. Her mother's family came from the Dominican Republic. Her father's family was from Puerto Rico. T. Q. was not happy at home. She complained that her younger brother was her mother's favorite. When she was fourteen, she began using marijuana at night in the park. One night, she met a man who was smoking crack. He told her that he had rented a room. He and his friends used cocaine there. T. Q. joined the group. She snorted cocaine for a while. Her nose became so irritated, though, that she had to stop it. Then, she started smoking freebase cocaine and became addicted.

T. Q.'s life became centered on cocaine. Her mother accused her of stealing money from her dresser. T. Q. left her mother's home and lived wherever she could. She

Snorting cocaine for an extended period can lead to irritation and damage to the nose.

went from crack house to crack house. One of the men she got mixed up with was killed. His body was dumped in back of a building.

People in crack-infested neighborhoods often feel it is not safe to complain about it. The landlord of a building near a crack house tried to get people to testify in court about the drug dealers. Everyone was afraid, however. They remembered the fate of a woman who led the fight against drug dealing in her community. She was killed by the drug dealers.[20]

Some Signs of Cocaine Use

There is no pattern of symptoms or behaviors that definitely indicates that a person is using cocaine. (It is not until that person ends up in an emergency room that it is evident.) A person may have some physical symptoms, however. Cocaine users, particularly heavy users, may complain about feeling run-down, of having a poor appetite, and of not sleeping well.[21] These symptoms, however, could also match those of people who are depressed. Severe nasal problems also raise the possibility of cocaine use. Finally, poor school performance, being absent from school, association with peers who are known drug users, and delinquent acts are signs of possible cocaine use as well as the use of other illegal drugs.

two

Stories of Cocaine and Crack Abuse

Many people have gone through difficult, sometimes agonizing experiences as a result of their cocaine abuse. Some of these people have written down their stories and published them. Others, like T. Q., told their stories to researchers who published them.

One of the first books presenting a personal story of cocaine abuse appeared about one hundred years ago. It was written by Annie Meyers, a Chicago socialite. It was called *Eight Years in Cocaine Hell*. Meyers related how she made daily purchases of a cocaine snuff. At the time it was sold legally over the counter and was inexpensive. The preparation had the harmless-sounding name of Birney's Catarrh Remedy. In time, Meyers became addicted to the drug. One day, she was desperate for cocaine and had no money to buy it. So she took scissors and pried loose a gold tooth from her mouth to sell so she could get money to buy the drug. Blood was still streaming down her face and drenching her clothes when she sold the tooth.[1]

It is a vivid account, but does it sound true? What do you think? It would be difficult for a reader to check on the accuracy of such stories. This raises an important point about stories of cocaine and crack addiction: Although interesting and often compelling, they are not like scientific articles. Those are carefully reviewed by other scientists before publication. Stories of crack and cocaine abuse are personal stories. They are the writers' version of events that they have experienced.

The Internet is full of stories that people have told about their cocaine (and other drug) problems. One young man related how he always kept cocaine around his home. The only time he did not have it available was when he could not afford to buy it. When he did not have

One of the first books presenting personal stories of cocaine abuse tells of a woman who was so desperate for money to buy cocaine that she pried loose a gold tooth from her mouth to sell for money to buy drugs.

cocaine, the drug was always in his thoughts. The urge to use cocaine was very strong. However, some of the effects of the drug were undesirable. He reported that using the drug ruined his sleep. The day after using cocaine, he could not work well. He also complained of constant sniffling and shaking hands. Moreover, his cocaine habit had left him socially isolated.

Addictions and Life Organization has a web site at <http://www.addictions.org/stories.htm> in which people tell about their addiction problems.[2] One young woman told about her life as a crack addict. She related how she had lost weight, was depressed, and had lost all her friends. A man told how he had been instantly hooked on crack. He smoked it every day. He became severely depressed. Crack took control over him. Since then, he has been clean for a while. He does not know, however, whether he will be able to stay off the drug. The temptation remains strong to use it again.

Some people who are dependent on crack end up like T. Q. They spend their time in crack houses. Others recognize that they need help and try to turn their lives around.

An attorney in his thirties had used cocaine for nearly three years. He began using the drug at cocaine-using parties. The host would lay out lines of cocaine on a table for his guests to snort. After a while, the man started buying cocaine on his own. He used it more and more. As his addiction grew, he spent less time at his job. He spent much of his time thinking about cocaine or recovering from cocaine-using binges. In six months, he spent $36,000 on cocaine. Snorting cocaine severely damaged his nose. He lost forty pounds. His marriage was in serious trouble.

With his life falling apart, he entered a hospital for treatment. When he began treatment, however, he still had hopes of using cocaine on a limited basis when he was released. The hold cocaine had on him was very strong. It took several weeks of being in the hospital before he accepted the idea that he would have to give up drugs altogether. At this point, he entered actively into the treatment program. When he left the hospital, he attended a cocaine recovery support group. He was able to resume his law practice.[3]

Kim is another example of a person who was able to work through the difficult problem of cocaine addiction. Kim's story appears in Vicki Greenleaf's book, *Women*

Marijuana is often one of the first drugs that teens will experiment with on their way to trying other dangerous substances such as cocaine.

and Cocaine: Personal Stories of Addiction and Recovery.[4] Kim grew up in a middle-class family in a southern city. Her parents were described as overprotective and controlling. Drug use may have been an act of rebellion on her part. At age sixteen she began using marijuana. She also tried other drugs, including LSD. Her drug use increased when she started college. She knew that her older brother was using cocaine. She wanted to try it herself. One day, a girl in her dormitory introduced her to cocaine. Kim snorted it and her life soon became centered on drugs.

She became more and more involved with drugs. Her life went on a downhill slide. Desperate for drugs, she took part in a robbery of a drugstore. Not long after this incident, she became deeply depressed. She left college and returned home. For months, she hardly got out of bed.

When she felt better, she found a job as a waitress. She moved out of her parents' home into a dingy one-room apartment. She felt lonely and began using cocaine daily. In time, she began to inject cocaine into her veins. To get money, she dealt drugs and stole. Finally, she was arrested with her boyfriend for forgery. When she was released from jail, she entered a drug rehabilitation program. Vicki was fortunate. With the help of the treatment program staff and a support group, she was able to break free of drugs. She returned to school and got a degree in nursing. She began working in an addiction recovery program, helping other people addicted to drugs.

Cocaine is an equal-opportunity drug. Cocaine abusers can be found among teenagers and young adults who have dropped out of school. However, abusers can also be found among the rich and famous. Three talented actors—River Phoenix, John Belushi, and Richard Pryor—have been among the many people who abused cocaine. River Phoenix and John Belushi died from the combined effects of cocaine and other drugs. Richard Pryor survived his cocaine abuse and wrote about it.

River Phoenix

River Phoenix was born to parents who had dropped out of society. They used drugs and became involved in a religious cult. When River was a young boy, the family moved to Venezuela in South America. River showed musical talent from a very young age. He played the guitar and sang. Eventually the family returned to America and went to Hollywood. There, River Phoenix began to find work in television and movies. He starred in such movies as Stand By Me and Running on Empty. His performance in Running on Empty earned him a nomination for an Academy Award. All this success came while River Phoenix was still a teenager.

Phoenix began to use drugs, including cocaine. People who knew him thought that perhaps his drug use was his way of coping. He was under a lot of pressure as a result of his soaring movie career. He used drugs for several years. Then one night, at a club called the Viper Room, he was offered cocaine by a drug dealer. He snorted it. Then he started shaking and trembling. He briefly passed out. When he left the Viper Room, he collapsed on the sidewalk. He was having seizures. His heart stopped beating and he died. The autopsy (examination of his body after his death) revealed that he had used large amounts of both cocaine and heroin. Traces of other drugs were also found.[5]

Stories of drug abuse due to the pressures of fame are not uncommon in the film industry.

John Belushi

John Belushi, a comic actor, was a member of the television show *Saturday Night Live*. He also starred in successful movies. At the height of his fame he died from mixing cocaine and heroin. He had worked hard to get where he was. Suddenly, in his early thirties, it was all over. His widow talked about how he had used cocaine in the past. During the year before he died, he started using it again. He began binging on the drug. He said he could control his use of the drug, but his wife told him he could not. Unfortunately, she was right. He may have thought that using heroin would ease the distress that can come with cocaine use.[6]

Richard Pryor

Richard Pryor has made more than forty movies. Before his movie career began, he was a stand-up comedian playing in nightclubs. When he was performing in nightclubs, he was introduced to cocaine. He was sure he was not going to get hooked. After all, he reasoned, some of his friends had snorted cocaine for years and they did not get hooked. Pryor was wrong. In time he was using freebase cocaine for several days in a row. It got to the point where he said he was no longer able to tell one day from another. He began to develop ideas that people were stealing from him. He also began to hear the voices of people who were not there. In this mental state, he set himself on fire. He ended up in a hospital burn center with burns from his ears down to his thighs. The most severe damage was to the upper part of his body, where he had third-degree burns. Even after this terrible experience, he began to use cocaine again. It was a struggle to get cocaine out of his life. Pryor talked about the death of fellow comic John Belushi. Pryor remarked that it could have easily been him instead of Belushi who died.[7]

three

Effects of Cocaine and Crack

Cocaine comes in the form of a white powder. The powder, however, may not always be pure cocaine. Dealers may "cut" (dilute) the cocaine by adding other substances. Things like baking soda or sugar can be added. This makes it look as if there is more cocaine than there actually is.[1] Even deadly drugs such as heroin may be added.

Cocaine can be introduced into the body in several ways. Over the years, snorting cocaine into the nostrils has been the most common method. Repeated use, however, can severely irritate the nose. A second way of using cocaine is to use a needle or syringe to inject the substance (mixed with water) directly into a vein. There are risks involved here, too. Acquired Immunodeficiency Syndrome (AIDS) has often been transmitted by drug users sharing needles.

The third, more recent method, is to smoke

freebase or crack cocaine. Cocaine in its normal state is difficult to smoke because it is destroyed at high temperatures. However, freebase cocaine and crack can be smoked.

Freebase and Crack Cocaine

Making freebase cocaine can be a risky process. Dangerous chemicals are needed. The whole experiment can go up in flames. Because making crack does not carry these risks, it is more widely used than freebase cocaine. Crack is made by mixing cocaine with water and

Chemicals needed to make freebase cocaine make the process very dangerous. Illegal labs like this one have been accidentally set on fire in the process of making freebase.

another common chemical. The paste that is formed is cooked, and it hardens into rocks. The rocks are burned. This process gives off smoke along with a popping sound. The user inhales the smoke into the lungs.

Once cocaine is in the bloodstream, the chemical quickly affects the brain. When cocaine is inhaled through the lungs, much more of the chemical will reach the brain than would with snorting. When crack is inhaled, the effects are felt almost at once. It takes ten to fifteen minutes for cocaine that is snorted to produce a peak high. It takes only a few seconds, however, for crack to have this effect.[2] However, the high from crack does not last long—about fifteen minutes. The crack user may have to take repeat "hits" of the drug to maintain the high. So crack requires a much higher dose of the chemical to reach the brain in order to stay high for the same amount of time. It also reaches the brain more quickly than cocaine that is snorted.

The Effects of Cocaine

Cocaine affects the pleasure centers of the brain, which, in part, produce the high. What is the high like? The word often used to describe it is *euphoria*—a feeling of extreme happiness and well-being. The user may feel very alert, energetic, and in high spirits. Sometimes, the high begins as an intense rush. Along with the euphoria, users may feel anxious, restless, and irritable. For many people, cocaine use is an intoxicating experience. It can become sharply etched in their memories. The desire to reexperience the sensations can lead to a strong urge to use cocaine again (and again). For some people, cocaine use increases. They may feel an overpowering craving to use the drug. Cocaine can be very addictive. Some

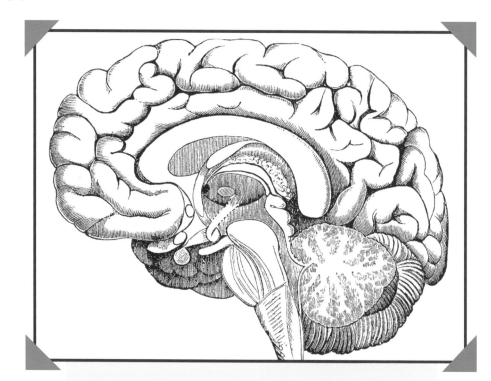

Crack and cocaine that are smoked reach the brain much more quickly than powdered cocaine that is snorted.

cocaine users go on binges. They may use the drug for hours or even days at a time. They may not eat or sleep during these binges. They can think only about using all of their cocaine until it is gone.

Cocaine acts as a painkiller. It causes a loss of feeling or sensation. For many years, cocaine was widely used to deaden pain in nasal surgery.[3] The drug is also a stimulant. Cocaine use quickens the pulse. Gabriel Nahas related the story of visiting a man in a New York City hotel room. The man had snorted cocaine, using a rolled-up one hundred dollar bill. Nahas could not stop him from using cocaine. Curious about the effects of the drug, he took the man's pulse. In two minutes, the man's heart rate had doubled, to 140 beats per minute.[4]

Cocaine also raises blood pressure and body temperature. These effects are likely to be mild when cocaine is snorted. They are greater when cocaine is smoked. The effects of the drug on the heart are complex. They are not yet fully understood. Cocaine use reduces the blood supply to the heart muscle. It can cause the

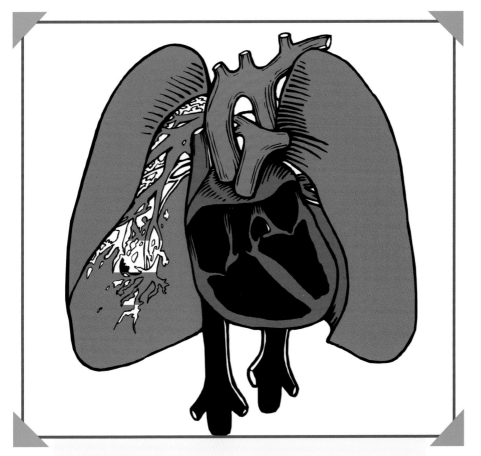

Cocaine and crack can damage the user's heart and lungs. Cocaine users are at increased risk for heart attacks, strokes, and chest pains.

muscular walls of the heart to become inflamed. It also disrupts heart rhythms.[5] Cocaine users are at increased risk for heart attacks and strokes. People who use cocaine often are probably most at risk for having heart attacks and strokes. However, some people have experienced strokes from a single use of cocaine.[6]

Smoking crack or freebase cocaine on a regular basis can also damage the lungs. A team of researchers at the University of California at Los Angeles studied heavy users of freebase cocaine. The people in the study often had coughing spells. These spells brought up black sputum—saliva mixed with mucus and pus—from the lungs. Study participants also felt chest pains when they smoked cocaine.[7]

Other effects of the drug that have been reported include seizures (as in the Len Bias case) and damage to the nose if cocaine is snorted. Nasal damage can be severe enough to cause collapse of the septum—the wall that divides the nasal cavities.[8]

Doctors at the Harbor–UCLA Medical Center in California have reported an epidemic of seizures in young cocaine users. It is believed that these seizures are due to the painkilling actions of cocaine.[9]

The Effects of Crack

A dramatic, though seldom reported, effect of smoking crack is uncontrolled muscle movements. After smoking crack, some people experience movements or shaking in their arms, legs, or head. They cannot control or stop these movements. This unusual reaction to crack cocaine has been called crack dancing.[10]

One daily user of crack was a thirty-four-year-old

woman. She had this problem for nine months. She also experienced lip-smacking and eye blinking.

Using crack can cause sores, blisters, and cuts on the lips and in the mouth.[11] Smoking crack has also been linked to eye damage. Researchers made careful eye examinations of about sixty people with a history of using crack cocaine. Defects were found in the nerve fiber layers of the retina. The retina, located in the back of the eye, contains light-sensitive cells. They act in a way similar to the way film works in a camera. The defects observed in the study did not generally affect the cocaine users' vision. However, the researchers advised their subjects to avoid further use of the drug. This would prevent more damage to their eyes.[12] There have also

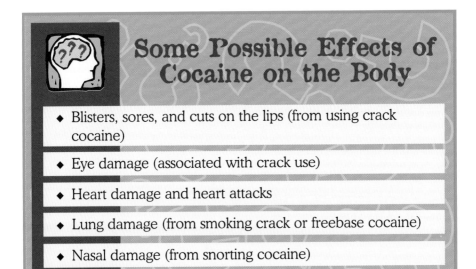

Some Possible Effects of Cocaine on the Body

♦ Blisters, sores, and cuts on the lips (from using crack cocaine)

♦ Eye damage (associated with crack use)

♦ Heart damage and heart attacks

♦ Lung damage (from smoking crack or freebase cocaine)

♦ Nasal damage (from snorting cocaine)

♦ Seizures

♦ Strokes

been reports of brain damage in people who use crack cocaine regularly.[13]

Psychological and Behavioral Effects of Cocaine

The main reason people use cocaine is to experience the high the drug produces. However, some more troubling reactions have also been reported. Heavy cocaine users have experienced a crash effect. After the high from the drug wears off, these users have experienced bad reactions. They may feel anxious, fatigued, and depressed. They need more cocaine to make them feel better. [14]

There are also reports that some cocaine users have become violent after using the drug. It is not clear exactly how often this occurs. In one particularly ugly incident, crack-using adults beat three young children to death.[15] There is some evidence to suggest that people who are already psychologically disturbed and use both cocaine and alcohol are high-risk candidates for violence. Researchers studied hospitalized psychiatric patients. About half the patients who had used both cocaine and alcohol thought about committing murder.[16]

The National Institute of Drug Abuse noted that "smoking crack cocaine can produce a particularly aggressive paranoid behavior in users."[17] Paranoid behavior is extreme suspiciousness. There is typically a belief that one is being persecuted. Evidence supporting this view comes from a study. Research subjects were given cocaine. They were then observed for evidence of guardedness and suspiciousness. The observers indicated that the cocaine users showed suspiciousness during cocaine use.[18]

Paranoid reactions to using cocaine appear to be common among longtime, heavy users of the drug. A study was conducted of a group of patients in a veterans hospital. They had used cocaine, on the average, for seven years. The study found that about three out of four of the patients had experienced episodes of paranoia after using cocaine.[19] Paranoid reactions often occur when the user is under the influence of the drug. The user seems to be looking for and finding threats in the environment where there are none.[20]

Experiments have been carried out to find out

Native peoples who live in the mountains of Peru and Bolivia (South America) believe that chewing coca leaves helps them work harder. The barrel in this photo is full of dried coca leaves.

whether cocaine affects a person's ability to learn and remember. There is some evidence that in large doses, cocaine use may lead to making more mistakes in learning new tasks. Researchers gave lists of short, made-up words like *pag* or *gic* to cocaine users before they used the drug. Afterward, the subjects were asked to type all the words they could remember. The subjects made more errors in this task after using cocaine.[21]

Cocaine is a stimulant. It makes sense to think that it might help maintain one's energy when a person would normally be tired. Native peoples who live in the mountains of Peru and Bolivia believe that chewing coca leaves helps them work harder. Research suggests that cocaine, like other stimulants, probably *does* have the effect of helping people resist fatigue—but at what price?[22]

Cocaine and Psychological Problems

Many people who are regular cocaine users have psychological problems. A study of high school crack users found that about one third of them had sought professional help for psychological problems during the past year.[23] The majority of people who called a crack hot line said they were depressed.[24] It is possible, however, that some of these people were troubled and depressed before they started using cocaine. They may have used drugs as a way of coping with their depressed feelings. It is also possible that the depressed feelings were brought on by the action of the drug. A drug-centered existence can destroy relationships and career plans.

Some cocaine users develop an interesting pattern of behavior called foraging. Foraging is a relentless search for pieces of crack cocaine that the user thinks he or she may have misplaced or lost. The searching behavior is compulsive. It is similar to that of a person who steps on each crack in the sidewalk while walking down the street. One man went to the emergency room stating that he was afraid of losing his mind. He was a heavy crack user. He smoked four to six hours a day. He spent a lot of time searching the carpet in the room where he had been smoking for pieces of crack. The man said that he knew there was no crack cocaine there. Nonetheless, he could not stop his compulsive searching behavior.[25] One woman went through a ritual of repeatedly checking her pockets, clothes, shoes, and socks. She was looking for cocaine that was not there.[26] The cause of this foraging behavior is not fully understood at this time. However, foraging is a common experience of people who have used cocaine heavily over a period of years. In research carried out with regular, long-term crack users, more than half the people studied reported episodes of foraging for crack.[27] Many of the users reported that they spent an hour or two at a time looking for lost bits of crack. And like the man who went to the emergency room afraid of losing his mind, some of these users reported that they could not stop themselves from foraging even when they knew there was nothing there.

four

Treatment for Cocaine Abuse

The goals for treatment are simple and clear: to help cocaine and crack abusers stop abusing the drug (and other abused substances) and stay off drugs. Other abused drugs are included along with cocaine because many, if not most, cocaine abusers also abuse other drugs. Continued use of any drug may increase the desire to use cocaine again.

These goals may be easily stated, but they can be hard to achieve. Help from trained people is often needed. For heavy cocaine users who are unable to stop, hospitalization in a drug treatment center may be required. Time away from one's usual environment in a setting that provides intensive care may be necessary. This is especially true for the person whose life has become centered on cocaine.

Treatment for cocaine abuse may include medications, individual and group therapy, and support groups. Drugs used to treat depression appear to help some people break the cocaine habit. Research indicates that some antidepressant medicines have been useful in reducing cocaine craving and use.[1] Although these drugs can be useful, they are not cures for the problem. As the public health service points out, "There are no known medications that prevent relapse to cocaine use."[2]

Both individual and group therapy may be helpful for some cocaine abusers. One of the biggest problems with therapy for cocaine users is that many patients quickly drop out of treatment. In one study, the patients quit group therapy after an average of six sessions.[3] That may not be enough time for therapy to be effective. When intensive group therapy was tried (the groups met five times a week), the patients attended many more sessions. The participation of someone close to the patient in the treatment process can also be very helpful.[4]

Relapse Prevention Therapy

One of the newer approaches to therapy for drug abusers is called relapse prevention therapy. The idea is to teach the patient how to identify high-risk situations that might lead to renewed drug use. They also learn ways of coping with these situations when they cannot be avoided.[5] Prevention techniques are used in drug treatment programs in many areas of the country.

Support Groups

Support groups for recovering cocaine users are typically based on the model developed by *Alcoholics Anonymous* (A. A.) These groups use a twelve-step program. It begins with an admission by the person that he or she is powerless to deal with the addiction. The addict must learn to rely on a higher power. Members of these groups meet regularly. New members are encouraged to attend meetings every day. New members may also be encouraged to choose a sponsor, a former cocaine user who is now drug free. The sponsor will work with the new member to help him or her stay drug free.

Two organizations that sponsor groups throughout the United States and Canada are Cocaine Anonymous and Narcotics Anonymous. Both groups try to provide an environment where recovering drug abusers can share experiences and help each other.

Drop-in Crisis Centers

Teenagers and young adults may not have easy access to treatment for their drug-related problems. They may really want help but feel reluctant to ask for it. Sometimes they may simply not know where to turn. Drop-in crisis centers can fill an important need for such young people.

Chabad House in Montreal, Canada, is a drop-in drug crisis center.[6] Chabad House is a Jewish service and educational organization. Its drug crisis counseling is free and open to all. At Chabad House, troubled young people come in when they are in difficulty. They may be welcomed with a good meal, understanding, and help to get them into a drug treatment program.

Beverly, a cocaine user, was upset and crying when she telephoned the house. She related how she had used freebase cocaine with her boyfriend. She admitted that she loved the drug. However, she said she would rather be dead than using anymore. The counselor talked her into taking a taxi to the house. There she joined three other young people. The ages of the four were fourteen, seventeen, eighteen, and twenty-one. With the counselor they talked, ate, and shared their problems. It was a long, draining evening. But there were no drugs used and no arrests were made. The young people were calmer. An opportunity was created to begin to do something about their problems.

Treatment for Teenagers

There are thousands of drug treatment centers in the United States. Some of these centers are connected with hospitals. Some are run by cities or counties. Some are run by nonprofit groups, and some are for-profit businesses. Only a fraction of these drug treatment

Support of family and friends is always very important and helpful on the road to drug addiction recovery.

centers have special programs for young people. A young person seeking a treatment center for cocaine abuse should find out not only whether the staff has experience in treating cocaine abuse, but also if the center has a program for young people.

Some hospitals have special units for treating adolescent health problems. Drug treatment programs for teenagers may also be run by youth service organizations in the community. One example is the Latin American Youth Center. It serves mainly the Hispanic community in Washington, D.C. The center has a drug treatment program that works with young people. Help is offered for drug problems such as marijuana and cocaine abuse. The program provides individual and group counseling. Family counseling is also available. The center has working relationships with neighborhood schools. The program helps find counselors for the young people. It also assists in dealing with legal problems that may have arisen as a result of drug abuse.

Some Suggestions for Treatment

Heavy users of cocaine may experience a number of physical symptoms when they stop. The urge to use cocaine may be particularly strong during the first week. Therefore, it makes sense to give patients extra attention during this period.

When patients are treated in the community rather than a hospital, urine samples should be taken at least two to three times a week. Patients' self-reports that they are not using drugs are not always reliable. People who are trying to stop cocaine use are cautioned to be on guard against exposure to people and situations that have

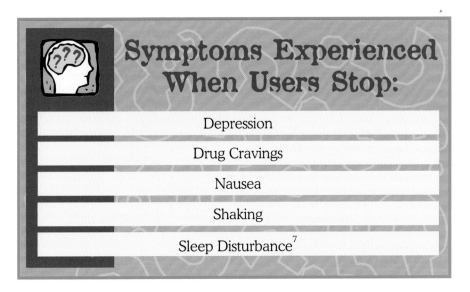

Symptoms Experienced When Users Stop:

Depression
Drug Cravings
Nausea
Shaking
Sleep Disturbance[7]

been associated with cocaine use. Such people or situations might trigger cravings to use cocaine.

Evaluation of an Alternative Treatment- Acupuncture

The search continues for new types of treatment. Some cocaine users have reported that acupuncture—the Chinese form of medicine that places needles into the skin in order to relieve pain—seemed to help them during withdrawal from cocaine. Researchers have carried out scientific studies to see whether acupuncture has any effect on cocaine use. When acupuncture was added to a standard therapy program, the patients stayed in the program longer. This gave psychological therapies more of a chance to be effective. Does acupuncture itself affect cocaine use? One study reported some possible positive effects. Another study found no effect.[8] Time will tell whether acupuncture can be helpful in the treatment of cocaine abuse.

Drug Courts: A New Social-Medical Approach to Treatment

The prisons in the United States are filled with thousands of cocaine users. Putting nonviolent drug abusers in jail, however, may not deal with their drug problems. Many communities have turned to a new, alternative approach called drug courts. When a person, often a teenager or young adult, is arrested for a drug offense such as using crack or cocaine, that person is given the choice between prison and the drug court. The drug court will often permit the offender to remain out of prison on the condition that he or she goes into drug treatment.

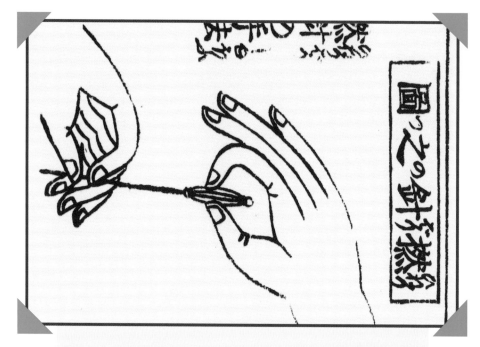

Some cocaine users have reported that acupuncture—the Chinese form of medicine in which needles are placed into the skin in order to relieve pain—seemed to help them during withdrawal from cocaine.

Treatment sessions are held often. Urine samples are routinely taken to make sure that the person stays drug free. If a urine sample indicates drug use, the drug court will impose penalties. These can include spending short periods of time in jail.

Drug courts offer a promising approach in society's attempt to better cope with the problem of drug abuse. However, as with any new approach that deals with medical and social problems, drug courts will need to be evaluated for their effectiveness.

five

Strategies for Prevention

Crack and cocaine can damage the heart and lungs, and can cause seizures. People have been paralyzed from cocaine-induced strokes. Others, like Len Bias, have died. Crack and cocaine can also create drug dependency. It is true that many people have used crack or cocaine once or twice and not become dependent on it. However, it is also true that many people have become dependent. Crack and cocaine can ruin lives. The smart thing is never to try either. More than nine out of ten teenagers do not touch them.

Strict penalties come with possession of cocaine and crack. Thousands of young adults are in prison today due to their involvement with cocaine and crack. Arrests for cocaine-related offenses are currently at about eleven thousand per year.

Sometimes people turn to drugs such as cocaine and crack as a way of coping with the difficult problems they encounter in everyday life. Cocaine and crack may seem to offer a way of solving these problems. In the long run, however, the drugs cause more problems than they solve. For people with problems that seem to have no solutions, a trained counselor can help.

Alternatives to Drug Use

Having enjoyable things to do can add meaning and satisfaction to life. This can act as an effective shield against experimenting with drugs. Participating in formal and informal after-school clubs and activities is a great start. There are many fun and interesting ways to interact with other people and feel good without the use of drugs.

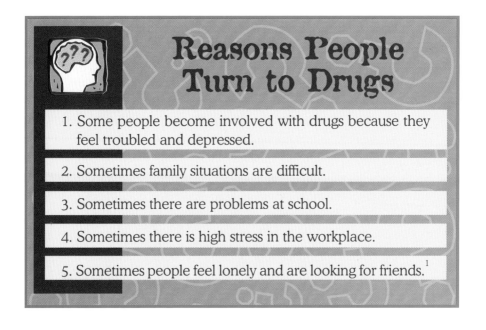

Reasons People Turn to Drugs

1. Some people become involved with drugs because they feel troubled and depressed.

2. Sometimes family situations are difficult.

3. Sometimes there are problems at school.

4. Sometimes there is high stress in the workplace.

5. Sometimes people feel lonely and are looking for friends.[1]

questions for discussion

1. Crack cocaine and freebase cocaine can both be smoked. Why do you think crack is more widely used than freebase cocaine?

2. The problem of crack babies has received a lot of publicity. What things could be done in your community to give crack babies the best chance for normal development?

3. The penalties for possession of significant amounts of crack and powdered cocaine are very different. Does this difference make sense to you? If yes, why? If no, why not?

4. Why do you think some teenagers become involved in selling cocaine?

5. Why is it difficult to use a person's behavior as the only indicator of whether or not a person is a cocaine user?

6. One of the approaches to treating cocaine abuse is to ask the user to attend many meetings with other people trying to stay off the drug. What do you think would be the advantages of this type of approach? What would be the disadvantages?

7. If a friend at school told you that he or she had heard that crack was safe to use, what things could you tell him or her about possible harmful effects of the drug?

8. If someone told you that most teenagers are using crack—that everybody does it—what would your response be?

9. Would you be in favor of having more drug courts in this country? If yes, why? If no, why not?

chapter notes

Introduction

1. Lewis Cole, *Never Too Young to Die: The Death of Len Bias* (New York: Pantheon, 1989), p. 70.

2. Ibid., p. 63.

Chapter 1. Society and Cocaine

1. Ronald K. Siegel, "Changing Patterns of Cocaine Use: Longitudinal Observations, Consequences, and Treatment," in *Cocaine: Pharmacology, Effects, and Treatment of Abuse,* ed. John Grabowski (Rockville, Md.: NIDA, 1984), p. 92.

2. Ibid., p. 93.

3. Frank H. Gawin, and Everett H. Ellenwood, Jr., "Cocaine and Other Stimulants: Actions, Abuse, and Treatment," *New England Journal of Medicine,* vol. 318, May 5, 1988, p. 1174.

4. "Cocaine Abuse," *National Institute on Drug Abuse Capsules,* Rockville, Md., January 1996, p. 2.

5. National Household Survey on Drug Abuse: Population Estimates 1995 (Rockville, Md.: Substance Abuse and Mental Health Services Administration, 1996), p. 29.

6. Robert L. Dupont, ed., *Crack Cocaine: A Challenge for Prevention* (Rockville, Md.: Office for Substance Abuse Prevention, 1991), p. 64.

7. "Cocaine Abuse," p. 1.

8. Dupont, p. 13.

9. Denise B. Kandel and Mark Davies, "High School Students Who Use Crack and Other Drugs," *Archives of General Psychiatry,* vol. 53, January 1996, p. 77.

10. Ibid., p. 76.

11. Paul Crits-Christoph and Lynne Siqueland, "Psychosocial Treatment of Drug Abuse: Selected Review and Recommendations for National Health Care," *Archives of General Psychiatry*, vol. 53, August 1996, p. 749.

12. "Cocaine Abuse," p. 2.

13. Reginald Smart, "Crack Cocaine Use: A Review of Prevalence and Adverse Effects," *American Journal of Drug and Alcohol Abuse*, vol. 17, 1991, p. 18.

14. Ibid.

15. Joan Biskupic, "Court Rejects Bias Claim in Crack Cocaine Sentencing," *Washington Post*, April 15, 1997, p. Al.

16. Ibid.

17. Terry Williams, *The Cocaine Kids: The Inside Story of a Teenage Drug Ring* (Reading, Mass.: Addison-Wesley, 1989), pp. 117–120.

18. U.S. Department of Justice, Federal Trafficking Penalties, January 1, 1996.

19. Terry Williams, *Crackhouse: Notes From the End of the Line* (Reading, Mass.: Addison-Wesley, 1992), p. 4.

20. Ibid., pp. 19–20.

21. Dale D. Chitwood, "Patterns and Consequences of Cocaine Use," in *Cocaine Use in America: Epidemiologic and Clinical Perspectives*, ed. Nicholas J. Kozel and Edgar H. Adams (Rockville, Md.: NIDA, 1985), p. 122.

Chapter 2. Stories of Cocaine and Crack Abuse

1. Annie C. Meyers, *Eight Years in Cocaine Hell* (Chicago: Press of the St. Luke Society, 1902), cited in R. K. Siegel, "New Patterns of Cocaine Use: Changing Doses and Routes," in *Cocaine Use in America: Epidemiologic and Clinical Perspectives*, eds. Nicholas J. Kozel and Edgar H. Adams (Rockville, Md.: NIDA 1985), p. 204.

2. Addictions & Life Organization, <http://www. addictions.org/stories.htm>, August 28, 1998.

3. Donald R. Wesson and David E. Smith, "Cocaine: Treatment Perspectives," in *Cocaine Use in America: Epidemiologic and Clinical Perspectives*, eds. Nicholas J. Kozel and Edgar H. Adams (Rockville, Md.: NIDA 1985), p. 194.

4. Vicki D. Greenleaf, *Women and Cocaine: Personal Stories of Addiction and Recovery* (Los Angeles: Lowell House, 1989), pp. 124–136.

5. John Glatt, *Lost in Hollywood: The Fast Times and Short Life of River Phoenix* (New York: Donald Fine, 1995), p. 267.

6. Judith Belushi, *Samurai Widow* (New York: Carroll & Graf, 1990), p. 106.

7. Richard Pryor, *Pryor Connections and Other Life Sentences* (New York: Pantheon, 1995), p. 203.

Chapter 3. Effects of Cocaine and Crack

1. Jay E. Rofsky et al., "Retinal Nerve Fiber Layer Defects and Microtalc Retinopathy Secondary to Freebasing 'Crack Cocaine'," *Journal of the American Optometric Association*, vol. 66, November 1995, p. 714.

2. Robert L. Dupont, ed., *Crack Cocaine: A Challenge for Prevention* (Rockville, Md.: Office of Substance Abuse Prevention, 1991), p. 6.

3. Reese T. Jones, "The Pharmacology of Cocaine," in *Cocaine: Pharmacology, Effects, and Treatment of Abuse*, ed. John Grabowski (Rockville, Md.: NIDA, 1984), p. 43.

4. Gabriel G. Nahas, *Cocaine: The Great White Plague* (Middlebury, Vt.: Erikson, 1989), pp. 5–7.

5. Allen Keegen, "Scientists Get to Heart of Cocaine's Toxic Effects on the Cardiovascular System," *NIDA Notes*, Summer/Fall 1991, pp. 21–23.

6. Bruce L. Miller et al., "Neuropsychiatric Effects of Cocaine: SPECT Measurements," *Journal of Addictive Diseases*, vol. 6, no. 4, 1992, p. 50.

7. Donald P. Tashkin et al., "Respiratory Effects of Cocaine Freebasing Among Habitual Cocaine Users," *Journal of Addictive Diseases*, 11:4, 1992, pp. 59–70.

8. "Cocaine Abuse," *NIDA Capsules* (Rockville, Md.: NIDA, January 1996), p. 3.

9. Miller, pp. 49–50.

10. Michael Daras, Barbara S. Koppel, and Elaine Atos-Radzion, "Cocaine-Induced Choreoathetoid Movements ('Crack Dancing')," *Neurology*, 44, April 1994, p. 751.

11. Sairus Faruque et al., "Crack Cocaine Smoking and Oral Sores in Three Inner-City Neighborhoods," *Journal of Acquired Immune Deficiency Syndromes and Human Retrovirology*, vol. 13, September 1996, p. 87.

12. Rofsky et al., p. 719.

13. James W. Cornish and Charles P. O'Brien, "Crack Cocaine Abuse: An Epidemic With Many Public Health Consequences," *Annual Review of Public Health*, 17, 1996, p. 265.

14. Marian W. Fischman, "The Behavioral Pharmacology of Cocaine in Humans," in *Cocaine: Pharmacology, Effects, and Treatment of Abuse*, ed. John Grabowski (Rockville, Md.: NIDA, 1984), p. 78.

15. Reginald G. Smart, "Crack Cocaine Use: A Review of Prevalence and Adverse Effects," *American Journal of Drug and Alcohol Abuse*, 17:1, 1991, p. 19.

16. Ihsan M. Salloum et al., "Disproportionate Lethality in Psychiatric Patients with Concurrent Alcohol and Cocaine Abuse," *American Journal of Psychiatry*, vol. 153, July 1996, p. 954.

17. "Cocaine Abuse," p. 3.

18. Michael A. Sherer et al., "Suspiciousness Induced by Four-Hour Intravenous Infusions of Cocaine: Preliminary Findings," *Archives of General Psychiatry*, vol. 45, July 1988, pp. 673–677.

19. Richard B. Rosse et al., "The Relationship Between Cocaine-Induced Paranoia and Compulsive Foraging: A

ChapterNotes

Preliminary Report," *Addiction,* vol. 89, September 1994, p. 1099.

20. Ibid., p. 1097.

21. Richard W. Foltin et al., "Behavioral Effects of Cocaine Alone and in Combination With Ethanol or Marijuana in Humans," *Drug and Alcohol Dependence,* vol. 32, April 1993, p. 101.

22. Fischman, p. 81.

23. Denise B. Kandel and Mark Davies, "High School Students Who Use Crack and Other Drugs," *Archives of General Psychiatry,* vol. 53, January 1996, p. 76.

24. Smart, p. 20.

25. Hani R. Khouzam et al., "Treatment of Crack-Cocaine-Induced Compulsive Behavior With Trazodone," *Journal of Substance Abuse Treatment,* vol. 12, March–April 1995, p. 85.

26. Ibid., p. 86.

27. Rosse et al., p. 1098.

Chapter 4. Treatment for Cocaine Abuse

1. *Drug Abuse and Drug Abuse Research* (Rockville, Md.: NIDA 1991), p. 118.

2. Ibid., p. 120.

3. Paul Crits-Christoph and Lynn Siqueland, "Psychological Treatment for Drug Abuse," *Archives of General Psychiatry,* 53, August 1996, p. 752.

4. Ibid.

5. Ibid., p. 751.

6. Chabad Project Pride, <http://www.chabadhouse. org/pride.html#about>, August 28, 1998.

7. See, for example, Mark S. Gold, Arnold M. Washton, and Charles A. Dackis, "Cocaine Abuse: Neurochemistry, Phenomenology, and Treatment," in *Cocaine Use in America: Epidemiologic and Clinical Perspectives,* eds. Nicholas J. Kozel and Edgar H. Adams (Rockville, Md.: NIDA, 1985), pp. 143, 145–146.

8. Alan J. Richard et al., "Effectiveness of Adjunct Therapies in Crack Cocaine Treatment," *Journal of Substance Abuse Treatment*, 12, November–December 1995, p. 410; D. S. Lipton, V. Brewington, and M. Smith, "Acupuncture for Crack-Cocaine Detoxification: Experimental Evaluation of Efficacy," *Journal of Substance Abuse Treatment*, vol. 11, May–June 1994, pp. 205–215.

Chapter 5. Strategies for Prevention

1. Drug Enforcement Administration, *Domestic Statistical Summary*, Washington, D.C.: DEA, 1995.

where to find help

Cocaine Anonymous
3740 Overland Avenue
Suite C
Los Angeles, CA 90034-6337
800-347-8998
<http://www.ca.org/>

Narcotics Anonymous
P.O. Box 9999
Van Nuys, CA 91409
800-338-8750
<http://www.na.org/>

National Drug Strategy Network
1899 L Street
Suite 500
Washington, D.C. 20036
202-835-9075
<http://www.ndsn.org/>

National Families in Action
Century Plaza II
2957 Clairmont Road
Suite 150
Atlanta, GA 30329
404-248-9676
<http://www.emory.edu/NFIA/>

Help Lines

National Clearinghouse for Alcohol and Drug Information
800-729-6686
<http://www.health.org/>

National Drug Information Treatment and Referral Hotline
800-662-HELP

glossary

Acquired Immunodeficiency Syndrome (AIDS)—A deadly disease of the immune system for which there is no known cure.

acupuncture—The Chinese form of medicine in which needles are placed into the skin in order to relieve pain.

Alcoholics Anonymous—A support group that uses a twelve-step program to help alcoholics stop drinking. The program begins with an admission by the drinker that he or she is powerless to deal with the addiction.

black sputum—Saliva mixed with mucus and pus.

cardiopulmonary resuscitation (CPR)—The life-saving method of applying pressure to the chest and breathing into the mouth.

crack—A form of cocaine that, when heated, hardens into rocks that are burned. The process of burning gives off smoke along with a "cracking" sound.

"crack dancing"—An unusual reaction to crack cocaine in which movements or shaking in the arms, legs, or head cannot be controlled.

"cut"—When used in reference to illegal drug making, it refers to the process of diluting the drug with another substance.

euphoria—A feeling of extreme happiness and well-being.

foraging—A relentless, compulsive search for pieces of crack cocaine that the user thinks he or she may have misplaced or lost.

61

freebase—A form of cocaine that, through a dangerous chemical process, can be smoked.

paranoia—Extreme suspiciousness.

relapse prevention therapy—A type of therapy that teaches patients how to identify high-risk situations that might lead to renewed drug use. Patients also learn ways to cope with these situations when they cannot be avoided.

retina—The area located toward the back of the eye that contains light-sensitive cells.

seizure—A sudden attack.

septum—The wall that divides the nasal cavities.

further reading

Carroll, Marilyn. *Cocaine and Crack*. Springfield, N.J.: Enslow Publishers, Inc., 1994.

Dupont, Robert L., ed. *Crack Cocaine: A Challenge for Prevention*. Rockville, Md.: Office of Substance Abuse Prevention, 1991.

Greenleaf, Vicki D. *Women and Cocaine: Personal Stories of Addiction and Recovery*. Los Angeles: Lowell House, 1989.

Herscovitch, Arthur G. *Cocaine: The Drug and the Addiction*. Lakeworth, Fla.: Gardner Press, 1996.

Kendall, Sarita H. *Cocaine*. Chatham, N.J.: Raintree Steck-Vaughn Publishers, 1991.

McFarland, Rhoda. *Cocaine*. New York: Rosen Publishing Group, Inc., 1997.

Nuckols, Cardwell C. *Cocaine: From Dependency to Recovery*. Blue Ridge Summit, Pa.: Tab Books, 1987.

Washton, Arnold M. *Cocaine Addiction: Treatment, Recovery and Relapse Prevention*. New York: Norton, 1989.

Williams, Terry. *The Cocaine Kids: The Inside Story of a Teenage Drug Ring*. Reading, Mass.: Addison-Wesley, 1989.

Internet Addresses

Cocaine
<http://www.nationalcounseling.com>

Cocaine/Crack: Negative Effects
<http://www.drugfreeamerica.org/>

Overcoming Crack/Cocaine Addiction
<http://www.crackbusters.com/>

index